SUSAN BUTCHER

THE ACHIEVERS

SUSAN BUTCHER

SLED DOG RACER

Ginger Wadsworth

Lerner Publications Company ■ Minneapolis

35834

When I decided to write about Susan Butcher, I contacted her for an interview, but she declined. My main sources of information were magazine articles, newspaper articles, books—including a guide to dog mushing, television coverage of the Iditarod Trail Sled Dog Race, and two articles in Susan Butcher's voice.

G.W.

LIBRARY OF CONGRESS CATALOGING-IN-PUBLICATION DATA

Wadsworth, Ginger.
  Susan Butcher, sled dog racer / Ginger Wadsworth.
    p. cm—(The Achievers)
  ISBN 0-8225-2878-9
    1. Butcher, Susan—Juvenile literature. 2 Iditarod Sled Dog Race, Alaska—History—Juvenile literature. 3. Women mushers-Alaska—Biography—Juvenile literature. 4. Mushers—Alaska-Biography—Juvenile literature. [1. Butcher, Susan. 2. Mushers. 3. Women—Biography. 4 Iditarod Trail Sled Dog Race, Alaska.]
  I. Title. II. Series.
  SF440.15.B88W34   1994
  799'.8—dc20   93-36093
  [B]   CIP
                                                                AC

Manufactured in the United States of America

1 2 3 4 5 6 – I/JR – 99 98 97 96 95 94

Contents

Susan Butcher and her dogs race across Norton Sound.

Dash to Nome

Susan Butcher and her dogs were running with the leaders. The team had completed nearly two-thirds of the Iditarod Trail Sled Dog Race across Alaska.

It was night. A thick cover of clouds hid the moon. Susan, wearing a headlamp that cast a tunnel-shaped light, decided to take a shorter, more dangerous route across Norton Sound, a frozen part of the sea. If she slipped ahead of the leaders, she might win.

She told the dogs to trot. Ahead, Susan glimpsed the huge expanse of empty ice and snow, polished smooth by the wind. Suddenly, beneath her, the ice rocked and rolled. In a split second, Susan, the dogs, and the sled tipped into a hole. Dangerously cold salt water surrounded her. Susan clung to the sled. She had only minutes to escape.

Granite, Susan's lead dog, dug his toenails into the solid ice at one edge of the hole. With powerful muscles from months of training, Granite pried himself onto the ice. He kept pulling. The rest of the team clambered onto the ice, followed by the 150-pound sled and Susan.

The dogs shook off the water, protected by their thick, water-resistant coats. But Susan could not stop shivering. She knew she had to act quickly. Telling her dogs to lope, or run, she turned the team toward the beach and solid ground. For a few hours, she ran behind the sled until she was finally warm.

Susan had been on the 1,049-mile trail nearly 20 hours a day for more than two weeks. Her team placed second, beating 53 other teams. She had nearly drowned in Norton Sound. But already, she was thinking about next March, about the 1985 Iditarod race. She and Granite would be back. Next time, she intended to win, even if she had to take more risks.

2

Setting Sail

Susan Butcher was born the day after Christmas in 1954. She grew up in Cambridge, Massachusetts, outside of Boston. She lived with her parents, Charlie and Agnes Butcher, and a sister, Kate, who was a year older. In 1953 her only brother, Evan, had died of leukemia.

Susan's father headed his family's chemical-products company. Agnes Butcher was a psychiatric social worker. Both parents told their girls that they could do or become anything they wanted.

To support that philosophy, Charlie gave Susan and Kate a set of adult carpentry tools. He taught them basic skills like how to hammer nails, measure and saw boards, and use a screwdriver.

He also gave his daughters sailing lessons in Boston Harbor. The three of them spent a couple of years trying to restore an old sailboat. Susan and Kate learned to scrape, sand, and paint, and to patch sections of the hull with new wood, but they never made the boat seaworthy.

The family often spent summers in Brooklin, a small town in Maine. Just west of Acadia National Park, Brooklin sits on a point that juts out toward the Atlantic Ocean. The Butcher family sailed in Eggemont Reach and into other bays and coves.

As a child, Susan loved the rocky coast of Maine.

Susan thrived in the countryside surrounding Brooklin. When she was not sailing, she tromped through the woods or explored tidal marshes.

In contrast, she hated Cambridge most of the time. She talked of tearing down her parents' city home and replacing it with a tiny log cabin surrounded by grass and open space. When she was eight, she wrote a school essay that started with the sentence, "I hate the city." She finished her paper by saying that she loved all animals.

She did like Cambridge when Mother Nature produced a powerful rain or snowstorm. Susan loved lightning and thunder, and would run out into the storm with her dog and best friend, Cabee, a Labrador mix.

Her parents were divorced when she was 11, and Susan's world turned upside down. Her father moved out, and Agnes Butcher raised her daughters alone. More than ever, Susan turned to Cabee and the neighborhood dogs for their unchanging love. After the divorce, she did not trust adults. She would rather be with her beloved animals.

Kate was also affected by the divorce. She often ran away from home. By the time she was 15, Kate had permanently moved out.

Susan continued to live with her mother, but like Kate, she was strong-willed. Mother and daughter clashed frequently. And school was hard, too.

Susan's teachers could not understand why she excelled in math but failed when she had to read or write.

After entering junior high, Susan was tested for learning disabilities. The tests revealed that Susan had dyslexia. When Susan read "pat," her brain might understand it as "tap." At that time, teachers were just beginning to learn about dyslexia. They knew that people with dyslexia were usually very smart, just like Susan, yet they needed help unscrambling printed words and phrases.

Susan earned A's and B's in science and studied college-level math. With tutoring, she struggled through English classes and others that required extra reading.

Yet school was not all bad. In high school, she discovered that she was a natural at sports. Because she was physically strong and determined to succeed, she became a star in softball, basketball, and field hockey. She loved swimming and school-sponsored rowing outings in Boston Harbor. She continued to sail and thrilled at taking risks in rough seas that kept other classmates on the beach.

When Susan was 15, Cabee died. A few months later, her aunt gave her a husky. They were a perfect match. Huskies are hardy dogs who enjoy exercise, especially in the winter.

A pure-bred Siberian husky pup

Susan named her new dog Manganak, for Zachary Manganak, a Native Canadian she had read about. When she bought a second husky, her mother protested, saying she did not want two dogs in the house. Susan took off for a while with her dogs.

Once, she traveled north to Nova Scotia, where she learned to farm and train horses. She always managed to find food and shelter for herself and her dogs. Along the way, Susan increased her carpentry skills. For a while, she thought she wanted to build wooden boats. She considered sailing around the world to get away from people but knew her dogs would not be happy on a small boat.

After high school, Susan and her dogs headed west for the open spaces of Colorado, where her father and stepmother lived. In Colorado, she met a woman who bred and raced about 50 sled dogs. Susan moved in with her and helped with the dogs' care and training.

Borrowing her roommate's dogs, Susan began to mush, or drive a sled with a team of 3 to 20 dogs through the snow. Susan learned how to work with a sled, keeping it upright on a bumpy path, or steering it around fallen trees and rocks. She was called a musher, and one of her many jobs was to guide the dogs by voice commands. On the weekends, she and other mushers competed in sled dog races.

For two years, Susan worked as a veterinary technician and mushed in Colorado. She loved dog mushing and was good at it. She had an unusually strong heart and lungs. She also had naturally warm hands and feet, a strong grip, and flexible joints and spine, which would help her as the sled bounced over the rough land.

By the age of 19, Susan knew that she wanted to live in the wilderness with lots of dogs. Colorado seemed too crowded. One of her dogs was stolen.

The other was killed by a car. Susan considered moving to western Canada.

An article in a dog-mushing magazine helped her change her mind. That year, 1973, was the first annual running of a sled dog race in Alaska called the Iditarod Trail Sled Dog Race, or the Last Great Race on Earth. Before long, Susan was on her way to Alaska, with dreams of owning and running a team of dogs in the Iditarod.

A small Siberian husky team takes off through the woods.

Susan feeds her hungry Alaskan huskies.

North to Alaska

Susan, who was just 20, found several jobs in Alaska. In the fish canneries, she cleaned salmon. At the University of Alaska in Fairbanks, she worked as a veterinary technician. She also helped deliver baby musk-oxen at a campus farm.

During her first months in Alaska, Susan acquired three Alaskan huskies from the same litter. She named one Tekla. She picked Tekla and the other animals carefully, seeking dogs with both character and heart.

Whenever she earned a little extra money, Susan bought another dog. After living in the city of Fairbanks for a while, she decided to move to the wilderness during the winter. She wanted to establish a close relationship with her puppies.

She also wanted to learn survival techniques, because she would be miles from the nearest hospital. Drownings, fatal plane accidents, and other kinds of accidental deaths are common in Alaska. Susan had to learn self-reliance.

She selected a spot in the Wrangell Mountains near the Canadian border in southern Alaska. A small plane dropped Susan, her dogs, and her supplies near a small log cabin in the bush—a large, uncleared, unpopulated area.

She lived in the cabin, 50 miles from the nearest dirt road. The house had no plumbing or electricity. At the nearby creek, she chopped a hole in the ice. She hauled icy water to the cabin to use for drinking, washing, and cooking. She cut her own firewood. When she needed food, she killed moose, caribou, and other wild animals for herself and her dogs.

Seven days a week, Susan rose by 5:30 A.M. and started a fire in the wood-burning stove. She dressed quickly in jeans and a shirt. She neatly braided her waist-long hair in one or two dark brown braids, then pulled on knee-high rubber boots and a parka before going outside.

Susan greeted each pup by name. Each pup got a hug or a pat. They romped with Susan and licked her face. She talked gently to them and even sang to them.

Two-month-old Alaskan huskies—future sled dogs—are comfortable around sleds from the beginning.

In the wild, dogs live in packs. The strongest dog is the leader. Susan wanted the pups to accept her as the leader, or alpha dog. They began to bond to Susan's touch, smell, and presence. She became their leader and the most important person to them in both work and play.

By the time the pups were four months old, they could walk several miles a day with Susan. They liked to splash through creeks, climb over rocks and logs, and run up and down banks. They had long legs and slim bodies, and they loved to run.

19

Susan taught the dogs to share in the teamwork of pulling a sled. Voice commands were equally important. When Susan called out "Gee" or "Haw," the dogs had to respond immediately by turning right or left. It could be a matter of life or death. Susan's command might turn the team away from a cliff or a dangerous section of ice.

During the training runs, the dogs strengthened their lungs and developed powerful muscles. To be champion sled dogs, the huskies would have to be able to trot 12 miles per hour and to lope 18 miles per hour.

Susan had limited training on how to raise sled dogs. She simply did what she felt was right. Her goal was to be the best sled dog racer in the world.

For part of three winters, Susan mushed her small team of dogs in the Alaskan wilderness. She loved to watch her young team before her, silent except for the whuff-whuff sound of their breathing and the jingle of the snaps on their collars. Susan pedaled—pushing the sled with one foot while keeping the other foot on the runner— behind her team for miles on her sturdy legs. She stayed off the sled longer than most mushers, making the sled lighter for her dogs.

One November, she headed across the wilderness to a friend's house for Thanksgiving. Mushing her team of 12 dogs, she fell into some icy water. She was soaked. There was no wood to burn because she was high in the mountains above the line where trees grow. At dusk, she found an unused cabin. Susan pulled the sled and dogs inside. She peeled off her wet clothes, and climbed into her sleeping bag with four of her dogs.

Relying on the warmth of her animals and her bag, she survived the $-25°F$ cold, only to find her clothes frozen the next morning. She tore apart the cabin and burned the wooden boards to thaw her clothes. After that, she finished her trip, arriving a day late for Thanksgiving dinner.

After three winters in the Wrangell Mountains, Susan drove her car to Knik, a village 18 miles north of Anchorage. Knik is the site of the Mushers' Hall of Fame. According to one story, 15 Alaskan huskies filled her yellow Volkswagen bug.

Susan wanted to meet Joe Redington, the Father of the Iditarod. She knew of his legendary feats as a musher in Alaska. Redington had traveled more than 160,000 miles across Alaska with his sled dog teams, often rescuing survivors from wrecked bush planes. Susan wanted to learn from the best coach and musher available.

Under Redington's watchful eyes, she began to train some of his young dogs. He gave her two huskies for pay and let Susan pitch a tent in the woods near his kennel.

Joe Redington, the
Father of the Iditarod

As Susan added more dogs to her kennel, she needed more money for their food and her sledding equipment. Jobs were scarce and low-paying. Redington told Susan that she needed a sponsor.

Sponsors, such as clothing companies or dog food manufacturers, give money to athletes. In return, athletes often wear the sponsor's name on their clothing and help advertise their products.

Redington convinced two Anchorage television stations to film Susan in 1977. Wearing a bathing suit, she chopped a hole in a frozen lake and jumped in to the whir of cameras. The publicity—of how a musher supposedly stays clean—helped her get her first sponsor. At that time, Redington predicted that Susan would someday win the Iditarod. The mostly male mushers around just laughed.

Susan entered the Iditarod for the first time in 1978. She was just 23. The race began in Anchorage, the largest city in Alaska, with a population of about 200,000 people.

According to the rules, each musher could use up to 20 dogs. Some mushers started with less than 20 because of the way their dogs worked together. Two nights before the race, the mushers drew times for the staggered start.

On the first Saturday in March, a rowdy crowd lined both sides of Fourth Street. One by one, teams of yowling, excited dogs left the downtown at two-minute intervals to starting commands of "Mush!" "Hike!" "All Right!" "Let's Go!"

From Anchorage, each team mushed for 20 miles on city bike paths to Eagle River, the first checkpoint. After Settler's Bay, the mushers left the highways and bustling activity surrounding Anchorage. The trail headed into remote Alaska. They traveled to Skwentna. They crossed over the Alaska Range at Rainy Pass, 3,160 feet high. On the other side of the Alaskan Range, Susan and her team reached the Kuskokwim River.

According to the Iditarod rules, Susan had to stop at dozens of checkpoints along the route. Veterinarians examined each dog for health problems. Injured dogs could be dropped from the team but not replaced.

At one of the checkpoints, the mushers and their
dogs were required to sleep and rest for 24 hours.
The dogs curled up in a ball and covered their faces
with their bushy tails. They slept, often hidden by
drifting snow. Susan used some of the time to mend
harnesses before dozing for a few hours.

24

THE IDITAROD TRAIL

During Alaska's gold rush in the early 1900s, the Iditarod Trail was used as a freight route. The trail was named after the town of Iditarod, which means a far distant place. Mail and supplies were delivered to Iditarod and other mining camps by dog sled. Gold came out, also by dog sled. After the gold rush ended, the trail was seldom used. Iditarod became a ghost town.

In the winter of 1925, an epidemic of the deadly disease, diphtheria, broke out in Nome. The closest serum, or medicine, was in Anchorage. The serum was shipped by railroad to Nenana, southwest of Fairbanks. Twenty sled dog mushers and their dogs took part in the dramatic relay "race against death" from Nenana to Nome. The last driver, Gunnar Kaasen, and his lead dog, Balto, delivered the life-saving serum to Nome.

To honor the serum run, the Iditarod Trail Sled Dog Race was organized in 1973. The 1,049-mile-long race begins in Anchorage and ends in Nome, taking from 11 to 32 days to complete, depending on the weather. The trail crosses two mountain ranges, winds over 200 miles along the Yukon River, goes through tundra, forests, across sea ice, farms, fields, and through tiny communities.

Many of the people in the small towns along the trail, like the old mining camps of Ophir and Ruby, eagerly awaited the arrival of the mushers. Dozens of ham radio operators—often providing the only communication among the villages—updated the residents on the race.

In the interior villages, old-timers relived earlier sled dog races. Residents rode out on snowmobiles to greet the approaching racers. They prepared feasts of reindeer steak, moose stew, and sourdough pancakes to refuel the mushers.

Susan was exhausted. Her eyes were tired and wind-blown snow had scratched her eyelids. Days of cold had shriveled the inside of her nose.

Dog teams are bedded down on river ice for a short rest at the Skwentna checkpoint.

A sled dog curls up in a ball to sleep.

Following a brief nap, Susan returned to the trail. Finally, she reached the coast. On the last stretch, Susan switched to a lighter sled, which she had stashed before the race. She and her team sprinted toward Nome, a former gold rush town with a population of 4,000. After going about 1,100 miles, she and her dogs crossed under the wooden arch that marks the end of the race in Nome. Susan looked forward to her first bath in two weeks.

She was pleased with her race. She had finished in 19th place. Only the first 20 mushers into Nome earned prize money. Susan used some of her $600 prize money to buy another dog. This dark gray dog had unusually thick fur. He weighed 58 pounds, which was big for an Alaskan husky. She hoped he would father champion sled dogs. Susan named him Granite.

Susan and her team are met by local children as they
lead another team into Koyuk during the Iditarod.

Breaking the Trail

Susan came in ninth in the 1979 Iditarod, reaching the end of the trail in 16½ days. She was 19 minutes ahead of her teacher and coach, Joe Redington, who came in tenth.

After the 1979 Iditarod, Susan assembled a new team of dogs with Joe Redington and his family. For fun, they spent 40 days climbing Denali, the highest mountain peak in North America. They were the first people to mush to its summit.

Life was not all fun. Susan's debts grew as she bought more dogs. Equipment broke. After working at a fish cannery, she often slept in her car or at a friend's apartment.

About 60 mushers and teams started the Iditarod in 1980, including Susan, who had just turned 25. Only a few of the mushers were women.

Susan cares for her dog team at the Iditarod checkpoint.

Susan and her dogs often ran for eight hours at a stretch. When the dogs grew hungry, Susan stopped and heated water on a portable stove. Each dog needed about 8,000 calories of high-energy food a day. Susan cooked a stew of beef, beaver, liver, salmon, bacon, and seal blubber. She could not keep her gloves off for long. The freezing temperatures made her hands susceptible to frostbite.

At the checkpoints, Susan massaged her dogs' sore shoulders. She rubbed ointment into and between their paw pads. Sometimes the ointment had frozen solid, so Susan had to thaw it first on her stove. Before going on, she might rearrange her team in their harnesses or drop a dog from the team if it was ill or injured.

When Susan called her dogs, telling them it was time to go, they began to yelp and yowl. They were eager to return to the trail.

Susan was on the trail nearly 20 hours each day. She and her dogs ran day and night. At night, she wore a headlamp. In front of and behind her, she could see the dots of other headlamps and hear mushers urging their teams on through the dark.

She guided her team past trees, rocks, and ice formations that looked scary in the darkness. Ice crystals gathered on her fur-trimmed parka. She pulled a wool mask over her nose and mouth. Sometimes she saw people and trees that did not exist. But Susan knew that lack of sleep caused these hallucinations.

Susan came in fifth in 1980, completing the course in 15 days and bringing home $3,000 in prize money.

After the race, Susan thought she had a $15,000 sponsorship deal lined up. She charged $6,000 worth of dog food from a young salesman, David Monson. When the sponsor backed out, Susan owed David Monson $6,000. Whenever she could, she paid David back in $10 and $25 payments. Although money continued to be tight, Susan scraped up the entrance fee to run in the 1981

Iditarod. Susan reached Nome in 12 days, 12 hours, and 45 minutes, again coming in fifth. This time, she won $6,000.

Susan and David became friends. By 1982 they were visiting one another and dating, despite a separation of 600 miles. Susan had moved to Eureka, Alaska, with her dogs—numbering more than 100. A tiny community of mushers and miners, Eureka is 140 miles northwest of Fairbanks and 100 miles south of the Arctic Circle.

She lived in a log cabin—built by a blacksmith during the gold rush—surrounded by run-down cabins and mining shacks. Her doorless outhouse sat 30 feet from the cabin. She had no running water or electricity. The creek was 1/4 mile from her cabin. Using her carpentry skills, she repaired some of the shacks. She named her new home Trail Breaker Kennels.

Susan lived four miles from her nearest neighbor. Most neighbors were seasonal miners who sifted the creek sand for flecks of gold during the summer. Manley Hot Springs, 30 miles away, had the nearest phone.

Susan had picked a part of Alaska where she could train right outside her back door. This part of the state has unusually strong winds and powerful snowstorms. Often, snow stays on the ground from early October through April.

Susan also wanted to work with Rick Swenson, who lived in Eureka and was the top long-distance sled dog racer in North America. A burly gold miner, Rick was the only person to have won the Iditarod more than once. He had his own approach to dog feeding and training. Susan and Rick Swenson, alike in their intensity and drive to win, became friends.

Susan started each morning early, hauling buckets of food to her dogs as she did several times a day. Afterward, she cleaned up after every dog and spread clean straw in the puppy dens.

Susan relaxes at home in her kitchen.

Because the nearest vet was several hours away, Susan did most of her own "doctoring." She drew blood, gave shots, tested urine samples, and learned to spot diseases. She treated minor injuries and simple diseases herself, and when necessary, sat up with a sick dog all night.

She helped her dogs with difficult births. Within a few moments of birth, before the pups started to nurse, Susan handled each dog. She stroked them with her fingertips, talked softly to them, and blew into their noses. She complimented the new mother for her beautiful puppies.

She gave each puppy a special name. Some were named for places, some for people, some for characters in books. One male was named Crackers, so his puppies were named after different kinds of crackers. The puppies quickly learned their names and came to Susan when she called them.

She kept a log for each dog, including a family tree. She recorded the dog's parents and grandparents. Susan knew which dog had a cold, which one did not eat well, and where each dog liked to be scratched.

Weaned from their mothers after a few weeks, the puppies lived together in a puppy pen. When they were a year old, they each got their own plywood doghouse—built by Susan.

In the autumn, Rick Swenson trains his dogs on an all-terrain vehicle, or ATV.

Susan divided the adult dogs into teams for training runs. She wanted them to run in teams three to five times a week. Before there was enough snow for real mushing, she hitched a team of three to five dogs to a 350-pound all-terrain vehicle, or ATV. Susan sat in the driver's seat. The dogs ran with the 490-pound load for four miles, at an average speed of 15 miles per hour.

Following the first heavy snowfall, Susan brought the sled out and harnessed the teams. In order to train all the dogs on a regular basis, Susan worked with four teams a day and covered a total of 70 miles. By the end of the day, her feet were often numb and her hands were red from the cold.

From the beginning, Susan studied the young huskies, looking for leadership traits, athletic ability, and a love of racing. She watched the experienced, older dogs to see how they worked with the younger huskies.

Tekla, one of her first huskies, became a strong lead dog. She had a good appetite and good feet. Tekla also could remember routes they had taken before, all-important during blizzard conditions when Susan couldn't see very far.

Some dogs could not handle the stress of being a leader, they worked well as team members. Some made great swing dogs, running directly behind the leaders. Other huskies became wheel dogs, running in front of the sled and pulling it out around corners and trees.

Granite was stubborn and slow to learn his commands. Susan worked with the big dog, giving him chance after chance to succeed. He had a great heart and lungs, and he loved to run. But he lacked confidence. Her philosophy was to give each of her dogs a second, third, or even a tenth chance to become a great sled dog.

Slowly but surely, Granite started to respond to Susan's love and gentle persistence. He learned his commands and did what Susan asked him. Although not aggressive, Granite was respected as a leader by the other dogs.

Susan chats with David Monson at the Eagle Island checkpoint.

Susan continued dating David Monson. By now David helped with the day-to-day running of Trail Breaker Kennels, and they both entered races.

Every year, Susan prepared for the biggest race, the Iditarod, which always starts in early March. A few weeks before the race, she began to pick her team, which would number between 15 and 20 dogs. By then, each dog had run more than 2,000 miles in training during the year.

In March 1982, Susan and her dogs arrived in Anchorage with David. More than 60 mushers, most of them men, had gathered there with more than 1,000 dogs.

In the first few miles of the race, Tekla and Ali, Susan's lead dogs, set the pace, pulling the 150-pound sled. They were followed by her spare leaders, Copilot and Beaver, Stripe and Dandy. Ivak and his son Ivar were the wheel dogs. Susan ran behind. Tipping their ears back, all 15 dogs listened for Susan's commands.

An hour into the race, the team hit an icy patch and slid into a fallen tree. Cracker, Ruff, and Screamer were too injured to run. Susan loaded them onto the sled, which now weighed close to 300 pounds. Instead of quitting, she returned to the trail. Before long, a violent snowstorm wiped out the course. Whiteout conditions, or swirling snow, made it impossible to see the orange reflector markers. Even the dogs were hard to spot. Susan veered 10 miles off course before finding the trail again with the help of Tekla and a compass.

At Skwentna, Susan left the three injured dogs behind so they could be flown home. Back on the trail, Tekla began to limp. She had reached her physical limit and needed to be dropped at the next checkpoint. For Susan, it was an agonizing decision because Tekla and Susan had learned how to mush together. Tekla had led her team in her first three Iditarods and to the summit of Denali.

With only 11 dogs, Susan continued toward Nome. Several days later, she made slow progress along Norton Sound. Shrill winds rose to 60 miles per hour.

Susan's clothes grew stiff with snow. The frost on her eyelashes and those of her dogs began to freeze their eyes shut. She stopped often to clear the dogs' eyes and to check their feet. The blizzard forced her to hole up in Shaktoolik, a town of about 160 people. To heat water and stay warm, Susan had to chop firewood in the now 80-mile-per-hour winds. Snowdrifts reached 30 feet in height. It was too cold outside even for the dogs, so they shared one small house with Susan.

When the storm let up, Susan mushed to White Mountain, 77 miles from Nome. Taboo, who became totally worn out from punching through heavy snow, had to be dropped. Susan had nine dogs left. During the last 22 miles of the race, Ali and Copilot were in the lead. Ali had raced to Nome before and sensed that he was close. Although Copilot was bowlegged and not too fast, he was a powerful lead dog. Susan made a kissing sound. Ali and Copilot dove forward.

Susan raced into Nome 3 minutes and 43 seconds behind the winner, Rick Swenson. Susan's second place was the best finish ever for a female musher. After racing more than 1,000 miles in 16 days, she collected $16,000. The prize money would go to dog food and new equipment.

Sled dogs strain to start running at the beginning of the
Iditarod in downtown Anchorage.

5

"Let's Go!"

Both Susan and David entered other sled dog races in Alaska—the Kusko 300, the Norton Sound 200, the Nushagak Classic, and the Yukon Quest International Sled Dog Race. Each race increased their mushing experience.

Susan entered the 1985 Iditarod, knowing she was mushing her best team in seven years of learning, breeding, and training. She felt she could win.

The first night was clear and cold. Heavy snow covered the ground. Susan led a pack of 61 other mushers. She pushed her team toward the fifth checkpoint. She mushed her team into a thick spruce forest. They trotted over a rise. A female moose appeared on the trail. The moose charged into the team, apparently believing the dogs were out to kill her.

The moose's long legs tangled in the team's lines.

Susan went after the moose with her ax, driving it away. The pregnant animal returned, slashing and stomping the harnessed dogs with her hooves. Susan's lead dog, Granite, lunged for the moose. He was thrown against a tree.

For 20 minutes, Susan waved and poked an ax at the angry animal. Luckily, another musher came by with a .44 revolver. He shot the moose, killing it instantly. By then, 2 of Susan's dogs, Johnie and Hyde, were dead, and 13 were injured. Susan dropped out of the race.

Out on the trail, Libby Riddles went on to become the first woman to win the Iditarod.

Libby Riddles talks with fellow musher Martin Buser.

Susan spent the next week in an animal hospital while her injured dogs mended. She grieved for Johnie and Hyde, and even had sympathy for the unfortunate moose.

A month later, Susan entered the Coldfoot Classic Sled Dog Race, which covers 350 miles in the Brooks Range. Granite, who had recovered from the moose attack, was her lead dog. At the start that April morning, the sky was a clear blue. The temperature registered at −30° F, warm for that area and time of year.

Susan crossed the finish line first, going the 350 miles in two days and 16 hours. She collected the first-place prize of $5,000.

It continued to be a busy year. In August, Susan and David were married in the dog yard at Trail Breaker Kennels. Rick Swenson served as Susan's attendant. His wife Kathy baked the wedding cake. Tekla and Granite were ring bearers. Susan now had that one close friend for life. Together she and David formed a partnership in friendship and in work.

With David's help, Susan was already training for the 1986 Iditarod. After long training runs, she invited a dozen or more of her dogs into their cabin each evening. Some curled up on the couch next to her. Others stretched out on the linoleum near the wood-burning stove.

David (left) and Susan train their sled dogs on the Bering Sea.

She massaged their sore muscles and talked to her dogs about the day's workout. When it was time to check their paws for injuries, some of the veterans, like Tekla and Copilot, automatically rolled on their backs, feet in the air.

Between training runs, Susan did paperwork for Trail Breaker Kennels in an old log cabin. Several dogs dozed on the floor while she worked.

During the long winter nights, Susan and David began the time-consuming task of checking all the sledding equipment. Sleds needed new plastic runners, bolts, lashing, and supply bags. The dogs needed new custom-fitted harnesses. Sometimes there did not seem to be enough hours in the day to get everything done.

After the first of the year, Susan put together her racing wear of hand-sewn parkas, snow pants, and boots. For weeks, she and her friends sewed a thousand dog booties to protect her huskies' paws from ice shards, rocks, and sticks.

By February Susan and David were filling about 75 burlap sacks with chunks of frozen dog food for the race. Susan rolled balls of ground beef, vegetable oil, vitamins, minerals, and honey. Other bags contained booties, batteries for her headlamp, snowshoes, an ax, a sleeping bag, and Susan's food. She arranged to have most of the 1,500 pounds of supplies left at checkpoints along the course.

Everyone agreed that the 1986 Iditarod would be fast, due to a hard and packed snow cover. Susan left Anchorage with 16 dogs and a carefully loaded sled. Mattie and Granite were in the lead. Granite set the pace, listening for Susan's commands.

Susan rests during a training run near White Mountain.

A musher races over Rainy Pass during the Iditarod.

At dusk on the first day, Susan was traveling a twisted, wooded trail that came to a fork. Granite chose the right fork, passing easily under a low tree. Susan lost control of the sled and smashed into one tree and then another. The team and riderless sled went tearing down the trail and were soon out of reach of Susan's shouts.

Susan eventually caught up with her team. Although she was bruised and her clothes were ripped, her sled was all right. She headed into Rainy Pass in the Alaska Range. She was the first musher over the pass, the highest point on the Iditarod Trail.

Her boots squeaked on the hard snow as she plunged off the pass, winding between tall spruce trees, jagged boulders, and onto a frozen creek. Suddenly, one of her dogs disappeared into a hole in the ice. Susan braked the sled and quieted the team. Quickly, she chopped a bigger hole in the ice, freeing the dog.

Susan continued on. In some places, there was no snow on the trail. She bumped over frozen grass and dodged tree stumps, rocks, and logs.

When Susan left Unalakleet on the coast of Norton Sound, she knew she might win her first Iditarod. From Unalakleet to Nome, she swapped the lead several times with Native Alaskan musher Joe Garnie. Rick Swenson was running third.

She planned her all-important strategy for the final stretch. She put Granite and Spoons in the lead. Copilot and Stripe took the swing position.

A few miles from Nome, Susan heard the fire siren wail to announce that the 1986 champion was near. Fifteen hundred fans began to rush to the finish line on Front Street.

Susan made a kissing sound, telling her team to run. Granite leaped forward. Susan knew that he wanted to win the race. She whistled. The team began to sprint, running faster than ever. The dogs seemed to shed their fatigue despite nearly two weeks on the trail.

On March 13, shortly after midnight, under a clear sky filled with a brilliant display of northern lights, Susan crossed under the Iditarod Trail monument with 11 dogs. Television cameras captured the moment she won the 14th annual Iditarod Trail Sled Dog Race. Susan set a record time of 11 days, 15 hours, and 6 minutes.

At the end of the race, Susan hugged Granite, Spoons, Copilot, Mattie, and the rest of the dogs one by one, congratulating them. Years of training and breeding had paid off. Susan had produced champion dogs who loved to run, and she was proud of them.

Susan hugs one of her dogs.

After the Iditarod, Granite, Susan's superhero, earned a new house, made from part of a wood-burning stove. His home was placed beside David and Susan's cabin. The other dogs continued to live farther away, chained to their simple plywood houses.

Susan used the $50,000 prize money to run her fast-growing kennel. She now owned more than 150 dogs. She continued to gather sponsors—a dog food manufacturer, an outerwear clothing company, and a hotel chain.

David managed Trail Breaker Kennels. It took hundreds of dollars a day to care for the dogs and maintain the sleds, trucks, and other equipment. David added diesel generators to power lights, a telephone, a fax machine, and a stereo system.

The list of chores seemed endless. They sold dogs to make money. Mushers would pay from $1,000 to $10,000 for one of Susan's dogs. Even at that price, Susan only sold animals who did not meet her Iditarod standards.

She enjoyed the music from the generator-powered stereo—ranging from Ray Charles to Beethoven to Jimi Hendrix—but she let David answer the phone and deal with business matters.

By choice, she separated herself from the noise and confusion of the world. Raising her dogs in preparation for racing was a full-time job.

Susan races into Nome.

Leader of the Pack

By 1987 the Iditarod was an international media event. Reporters from *Sports Illustrated* and "Wide World of Sports" flew in to report on the Iditarod. Other journalists came from Australia and Japan. Bush pilots flew up and down the trail, filming the race and calling in updates.

Susan won again in 1987 with Granite as her lead dog. Her picture appeared in magazines and newspapers throughout the world. She was in high demand on television talk shows. Granite also became a star. Journalists wrote long articles about him and began calling him Rambo or Super Dog.

That same year, Susan received the Women's Sports Foundation's Professional Sportswoman of the Year award. She and David traveled to New York to receive the award. Everyone wanted to see and meet the two-time, female winner of the Iditarod.

Her back-to-back wins created a furor over men and women competing against each other in the same sled dog races. Some competitors, like Rick Swenson, wanted a separate Iditarod for men. He suggested a system for the Iditarod that would allow mushers who weighed more—namely men—to run with more dogs than mushers who weighed less—women. That system was not adopted. After the 1987 Iditarod, Susan's friendship with Rick Swenson ended.

Despite the wins, this was a difficult time for Susan. Some male mushers resented the fact that Susan—as one of only a few female racers—had attracted journalists and television crews, which in turn made it easier for her to find sponsors.

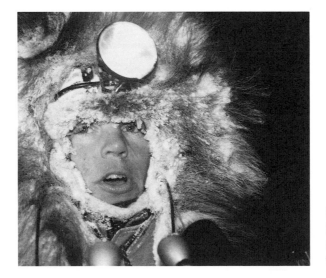

Susan is interviewed after finishing the Iditarod.

Some people also accused her of giving perfor-mance-enhancing drugs to her dogs. She denied these charges. Her dogs had always passed manda-tory urine testing during and following each race.

Susan responded that she was born with a special ability with animals and a particular love for them. She wants to bond with each puppy. This bond, not drugs, is what makes her dogs great. Often, mushers race with dogs trained by someone else. She raises every dog herself.

Susan refused to let anything interfere with her work. In her free time, she studied books about marathon running. She talked to other athletes and tried new training techniques on herself. All year long, she trained for her tenth Iditarod.

The 1988 Iditarod began as always, in downtown Anchorage. Fifty-three mushers and 869 dogs started for Nome. Although there was a lot of snow, the warm weather, with temperatures of 30° F and higher, created problems.

Susan's team, along with others, bogged down in deep, mashed-potato-like snow on top of Rainy Pass. On the backside of the Alaska Range, in Dalzell Gorge, her sled skidded sideways on some ice. It flew out of control and slammed into a creek, shattering a strut. Susan spent the next 24 hours fixing the sled with a pocketknife and a roll of duct tape.

She headed into the dreaded Farewell Burn, a 90-mile-wide stretch of fire-scarred and wind-scoured land. Her battered sled did not steer properly. Unable to stand on the runners, she ran beside her sled for the next three days, until she could replace it in Nikolai.

Halfway between Shaktoolik and Koyuk, Susan mushed her team through gale-force winds. Fine, hard grains of snow smacked her face. Her eyebrows froze white with snow.

The winds continued to build, spewing sprays of snow from every crest. Susan headed out across Golovin Bay. It required all her energy and dog-mushing knowledge to get through. Without Susan standing on the runners, the wind flipped her sled like a toy.

When she reached White Mountain, her right arm was numb and temporarily paralyzed from the cold. Susan went on the remaining 77 miles to Nome, with Granite in the lead. She won the Iditarod for the third time in a row.

Libby Riddles had won in 1985. Now, women had won the last four races. Once again, the media played up the male-female issue. T-shirt vendors sold thousands of shirts that read: "Alaska. Where men are men and women win the Iditarod."

Susan did not like being criticized because of her sex. She did gain strength, however, from women across Alaska who supported her. During the Iditarod, Native Alaskan women encouraged her as she passed through their villages, often saying, "Do this for us."

Susan entered the 1989 Iditarod, believing that her strongest competitor would be Joe Runyan, an Alaskan who had been mushing for nearly 20 years. She also would be watching Swiss-born Martin Buser, Rick Swenson, and several first-time mushers. A team of poodles ran that year. Each poodle wore a camouflage outfit.

Martin Buser shares candy with a Native Alaskan child at the Koyuk checkpoint.

Joe Runyan is ready to start the Iditarod in downtown Anchorage.

During the early days of the race, Susan's dogs came down with a virus that caused diarrhea. Susan sought the advice of several veterinarians and decided to treat the dogs with an antibiotic. The medicine did not help, and at one of the checkpoints, Susan dropped two of her sickest dogs.

In the frigid forests between the Kuskokwim and the Iditarod Rivers, Susan passed Joe Runyan and took the lead. She reached the tiny town of Cripple and won the Halfway Trophy and $3,000 in silver ingots. But Susan wondered if she were jinxed. Only once in the race's 16-year history had the midpoint leader gone on to win.

Later Susan was forced to drop two more sick dogs at Eagle Island. Every time she pulled into a village, children flocked around her, shaking her hand, seeking her autograph, and patting the dogs. For them, the Iditarod was the most important event in their year, except for Christmas. When she could, Susan dozed with a portable alarm clock balanced on her chest.

As villagers surround her, Susan tends to her huskies in White Mountain.

Back on the trail, Susan's strongest dogs could not stay in the lead. They were too sick. She ran Tempy and Lightning for only 30 or 40 miles, then switched to Sluggo and Elan.

Joe Runyan won the 1989 Iditarod. An hour and four minutes later, Susan crossed under the archway in Nome in second place. She was proud of her dogs and felt they had run their best race ever, despite their health problems.

Before the 1990 Iditarod, Susan entered six sled dog races, including the John Beargrease Marathon in Minnesota and the Coldfoot Classic in Alaska. She won four races and was second in two.

Seventy-two mushers, including six women, started the 1990 Iditarod. They had to deal with the deepest snow in 25 years. The weather was warm, reaching 40° F. Ash from Redoubt Volcano swirled through the air.

Ten-year-old Granite started as the lead dog. Two hundred miles into the race, he stepped into a deep hole, tearing a toenail. Susan had to drop him from the team, knowing this was his last Iditarod because he was getting old.

So Susan's fourth win came with a new lead dog, Sluggo, a honey-beige husky. She set a course record of 11 days, 1 hour, 53 minutes, and 23 seconds. Like Rick Swenson, Susan had now won the Iditarod Trail Sled Dog Race four times.

President Bush greets Granite and Susan at the White House.

After winning, Susan went east to meet President George Bush. Granite traveled with her. In Washington, D.C., he had his own hotel room. Fans addressed letters to "Mr. Granite." He ate ground beef served on a silver platter and drank bottled water from France. For the second time, Susan was named the Women's Sports Foundation's Professional Sportswoman of the Year.

During the summer, she crisscrossed the lower 48 states. She signed autographs, sat for photo sessions, and gave speeches. She appeared on "Good Morning America," "The Tonight Show," and "Today," and made advertisements for her sponsors.

Out in the dog yard at Trail Breaker Kennels, dozens of huskies saluted her return with yelps, yips, and yowls. Susan greeted her dogs one by one. In the kennel office, she outlined training schedules for the next year. She was eager to work with her top dogs.

Now, Susan had 20 to 30 retired dogs, including Granite and Copilot. That summer, Tekla died at the age of 15½. Even though Susan knew that Tekla would die one day, she was heartbroken.

Susan began to train for the 1991 Iditarod. She was going for an unprecedented fifth win. Susan believed her dogs were faster and stronger than any other team. She felt she could win. Near the end of the race, ground blizzard conditions kicked in. She could see only inches in front of her face.

Susan and her team race across Norton Sound out of Koyuk.

Susan chats with her friend and fellow musher Dee Dee Jonrowe during the 1993 Iditarod.

Due to the treacherous conditions, Susan turned back to the safety of one of the checkpoints. She finished third, and Rick Swenson won his fifth Iditarod.

Martin Buser won the Iditarod in 1992. Susan came in second.

The 1993 Iditarod was marked by new technology. Mushers used nonbreakable plastic sleds and carried satellite transmitters to pinpoint their location.

Susan left Anchorage with a team of 20 dogs. A heat wave had melted the snow, so the 68 mushers ran on snow dumped by trucks on the city streets.

Heading into the Alaska Range, the mushers encountered other problems. The melted snow froze at night, creating a glasslike surface. Sleds were hard to steer on the slick ice. In places where there was no snow, the sleds bounced over the exposed tundra.

Some of Susan's dogs grew sick. Others were injured by sharp bits of ice. Some had pulled muscles and torn toenails. She began to drop them at the various checkpoints. By Nikolai, Susan had only 11 dogs left.

Susan was exhausted. Too tired to find a real bed, she slept in the hay next to her team in Unalakleet. In Koyuk, 170 miles from Nome, the race was the tightest battle in years. Seven teams were bunched together. Susan dropped another dog. Two others were slowing down. She knew she had lost the race. Her only goal now was to finish.

The final part of the race was a two-way sprint between Jeff King and Susan's friend, Dee Dee Jonrowe. Jeff King won in a record time of 10 days, 15 hours, and 38 minutes. With a team of eight dogs, Susan finished fourth.

As always, journalists swarmed around the top finishers, demanding interviews. One person asked Susan about her future racing plans. She indicated that Trail Breaker Kennels would be back, with or without her as a musher. She had several talented young assistants who qualified as mushers to run the Iditarod. After all, she told the reporter, her dogs are the true athletes, the true champions. The musher is just their coach.

One of Susan's sled dogs rests in the Arctic sun.

At Trail Breaker Kennels, the air is quiet. The sun is out. Several dogs lie belly up, soaking up the Arctic sun. One of the huskies in the dog yard thrusts its muzzle toward the sky and howls. Other dogs howl, until all the adult huskies join in.

Susan Butcher leaves her cabin. She moves from dog to dog, dishing out breakfast, humming as she works.

Her head swirls with ideas, with dreams. Someday, she and David want to mush a team across Siberia. And build an animal research center. And start a family. In the meantime, 200 dogs expect and receive a greeting from their favorite person in the world.

Iditarod Statistics

YEAR	TOTAL MUSHERS	TOTAL WOMEN	WINNER NAME	DAYS	TIME HOURS	MINUTES	PRIZE MONEY
1973	34	0	Dick Wilmarth	20	00	49	12,000
1974	44	2	Carl Huntington	20	15	02	12,000
1975	41	1	Emmitt Peters	14	14	43	15,000
1976	47	0	Gerald Riley	18	22	58	7,200
1977	49	1	Rick Swenson	16	16	27	9,600
1978	39	3	Dick Mackey	14	18	52	12,000
1979	55	3	Rick Swenson	15	10	37	12,000
1980	61	6	Joe May	14	07	11	12,000
1981	53	5	Rick Swenson	12	08	45	24,000
1982	54	3	Rick Swenson	16	04	40	24,000
1983	68	9	Rick Mackey	12	14	10	24,000
1984	67	7	Dean Osmar	12	15	07	24,000
1985	61	4	Libby Riddles	18	00	20	50,000
1986	73	2	Susan Butcher	11	15	06	50,000
1987	60	5	Susan Butcher	11	02	05	50,000
1988	52	5	Susan Butcher	11	11	41	30,000
1989	49	7	Joe Runyan	11	05	24	50,000
1990	69	6	Susan Butcher	11	01	53	50,000
1991	75	6	Rick Swenson	12	16	34	50,000
1992	76	15	Martin Buser	10	19	17	51,600
1993	68	13	Jeff King	10	15	38	50,000

Susan Butcher's Iditarod Statistics

YEAR	PLACE	DAYS	TIME HOURS	MINUTES	PRIZE MONEY
1978	19	16	15	40	600
1979	9	16	11	15	1,600
1980	5	15	10	17	3,000
1981	5	12	12	45	6,000
1982	2	16	04	43	16,000
1983	9	13	10	25	3,200
1984	2	12	16	41	16,000
1985	Scratched				
1986	1	11	15	06	50,000
1987	1	11	02	05	50,000
1988	1	11	11	41	30,000
1989	2	11	06	28	35,000
1990	1	11	01	53	50,000
1991	3	12	21	59	32,000
1992	2	11	05	36	41,280
1993	4	10	22	02	32,000

ACKNOWLEDGMENTS

Photographs are reproduced with the permission of © Paul A. Souders, pp. 1, 6, 16, 26, 28, 30, 37, 40, 44, 45, 46, 48, 50, 52, 55, 56, 60, 61, 63; Tony La Gruth, p. 10; Lisa B. Fallgren Stevens, p. 13; © Margo Taussing Pinkerton / New England Stock Photo, p. 15; John S. Foster, pp. 22, 27, 42; Darren Erickson, p. 24; Sallaz / Gamma Liaison, p. 33; Reuters / Bettmann, p. 59.

Front cover photographs by Paul Souders.